THE BOOK OF
CONFIDENCE

For more copies of this book, please contact:

U.S.A. *$4.95*
America Needs Fatima
P.O. Box 341, Hanover, PA 17331
(888) 317-5571
www.ANF.org • ANF@ANF.org

Canada *Free*
Canada Needs Our Lady
P.O. Box 36040, Greenfield Park, QC J4V 3N7
1-844-729-6279 (1-844-Say-Mary)
www.CanadaNeedsOurLady.org
Info@CanadaNeedsOurLady.org

South Africa *R49.00*
South Africa Needs Our Lady
P.O. Box 141, Ladismith 6655
office@FamilyAction.co.za
087 230 9884
Banking details: FNB • 6251 606 5209 • Branch 200213

THE BOOK OF
CONFIDENCE

Father Thomas de Saint-Laurent

AMERICA NEEDS FATIMA
P. O. BOX 341
HANOVER, PA 17331
(888) 317-5571 • www.ANF.org

The America Needs Fatima Campaign is a special project of the
American Society for the Defense of Tradition, Family and Property
to win the heart and soul of America for Mary by spreading the
Fatima message. America Needs Fatima and the American TFP are
assumed names of the Foundation for a Christian Civilization, Inc.

Third edition
© 2015 by the Foundation for a Christian Civilization, Inc.
Sixth printing

Printed in U.S.A.
Library of Congress Control Number: 2015954788
ISBN: 978-1-877905-46-9

CONTENTS

CHAPTER ONE: CONFIDENCE!

♦ Our Lord Exhorts Us to Have Confidence 1

♦ Many Souls Are Afraid of God 2

♦ Others Lack Faith 2

♦ This Lack of Confidence is Very
Harmful to Them 3

♦ Goal and Content of This Book 5

**CHAPTER TWO: NATURE AND
CHARACTERISTICS OF CONFIDENCE**

♦ Confidence Is a Firm Hope 9

♦ Confidence Is Fortified by Faith 10

♦ Confidence Is Unshakable 10

♦ Confidence Counts on Nothing but God 13

♦ Confidence Rejoices Even at Being
Deprived of Human Help 15

**CHAPTER THREE: CONFIDENCE IN
GOD AND OUR TEMPORAL NECESSITIES**

♦ God Provides for Our Temporal Necessities 21

♦ God Provides According to the
Situation of Each One 22

♦ We Must Not Trouble
Ourselves about the Future 24

♦ Seeking First the Kingdom of
God and His Justice 27

♦ Praying for Our Temporal Necessities 28

**CHAPTER FOUR: CONFIDENCE IN GOD AND
OUR SPIRITUAL NECESSITIES**

♦ Our Lord Is Merciful to Sinners.....................33

♦ Grace Can Sanctify Us in an Instant 36

♦ God Grants Us All the Necessary
Helps for the Sanctification
and Salvation of Our Souls 37

♦ The Sight of the Crucifix
Should Revive Our Confidence 40

**CHAPTER FIVE: REASONS FOR
CONFIDENCE IN GOD**

♦ The Incarnation of the Word 45

♦ The Power of Our Lord 46

♦ Jesus Is Lord of the Supernatural Life 49

♦ Our Lord's Goodness 49

CHAPTER SIX: FRUITS OF CONFIDENCE

♦ Confidence Glorifies God 55

♦ Confidence Attracts
Exceptional Favors to Souls 56

♦ The Confident Prayer
Obtains Everything 58

♦ The Example of the Saints 59

♦ The Conclusion of This Work 61

NOTES 65

APPENDIX A

Trusting Through the Dark Night 73

APPENDIX B

Irresistible Novena to the Sacred Heart of Jesus 82

CHAPTER ONE
Confidence!

"If thou canst believe, thou shalt see the power of My Heart and the magnificence of My love."
—Our Lord to Saint Margaret Mary Alacoque

"And Peter going down out of the boat, walked upon the water to come
to Jesus. But seeing the wind strong, he was afraid: and when he
began to sink, he cried out, saying: Lord, save me."
—Matt. 14: 29-30

CONFIDENCE!

Our Lord Exhorts Us to Have Confidence

O Voice of Christ, mysterious voice of grace that resoundeth in the silence of our souls, Thou murmurest in the depths of our hearts words of sweetness and of peace. In response to our miseries, Thou repeatest the counsel so often given by the Divine Master during His mortal life: "Confidence, confidence!"

To the guilty soul, crushed by the weight of sin, Jesus would say: "Confidence, son, thy sins are forgiven thee."[1] Again, to the sick woman, suffering for long years from an incurable malady, who touched the hem of His garments in the firm belief that she would be cured, He said: "Confidence, daughter, thy faith hath made thee whole."[2] When the Apostles saw Him one night walking on Lake Genezareth they trembled with fear. He calmed them with these reassuring words: "Have confidence, it is I, fear ye not."[3]

And, on the eve of His Passion, at the Last Supper, knowing the infinite fruits of His sacrifice, He comforted the Apostles with these words of triumph: "Have confidence, I have overcome the world."[4]

These divine words, so full of tender compassion, as they fell from His adorable lips, effected a marvelous transformation in the souls of those to whom they were addressed. A supernatural dew transformed their aridity; rays of hope dissipated their darkness; a calm serenity put their anguish to flight. "The words that I have spoken to you, are spirit and life;"[5] "blessed are they who hear the word of God, and keep it."[6]

Our Lord exhorts us now, as He did the Apostles long ago, to have confidence in Him. Why should we refuse to heed His voice?

Many Souls Are Afraid of God

Few Christians, even among the most fervent, possess that confidence which excludes all anxiety and all doubt.

The Gospel tells us that the miraculous draft of fish terrorized Saint Peter. With his habitual impetuosity, he measured at a glance the infinite distance that separated his own littleness from the greatness of Our Lord. He trembled with holy fear and prostrated himself with his face to the ground, crying out: "Depart from me, for I am a sinful man, O Lord."[7]

Like the Apostle, some souls have this terror. They feel their sinfulness and their misery so keenly that they scarcely dare approach Him Who is Holiness itself. To them it seems that the all-holy God must experience revulsion upon inclining Himself toward them. This unhappy impression hampers their interior life and at times paralyzes it completely.

How mistaken are these souls!

Immediately, Jesus approached the frightened Apostle and said to him, "Fear not,"[8] and made him rise.

You also, Christians, you who have received so many proofs of His love, fear not! Above all, Our Lord is concerned that you might fear Him. Your imperfections, your weaknesses, your most serious faults, your repeated relapses, nothing will discourage Him, so long as you sincerely wish to repent. The more miserable you are, the more He has pity on your misery, the more He desires to fulfill His mission of Savior in your regard. Was it not above all to call sinners that He came to the earth?[9]

Others Lack Faith

Other souls lack faith. They, of course, have that common faith, without which they would betray the grace of Baptism. They believe that Our Lord is all-powerful, good, and faithful to His promises. But they find it hard to believe that He is concerned about their individual necessities. They do not have the irresistible conviction that God, mindful of their trials, is watching over them, ever ready to help them.

Our Lord asks of us, however, this special concrete faith. He exacted it of old as the indispensable condition for His miracles; He still expects it of us before granting us His favors.

"If thou canst believe, all things are possible to him that believeth,"[10] He said to the father of the possessed boy. And, in the convent of Paray-le-Monial, using almost the same words, He said to Saint Margaret Mary: "If thou canst believe, thou shalt see the power of My Heart and the magnificence of My love."

Can you believe? Can you attain that certainty which is so strong that nothing shakes it, so clear that it amounts to evidence? This is everything. When you reach this degree of confidence, you will see wonders realized in you. Beseech, therefore, the Divine Master to increase your faith. Repeat often the prayer of the Gospel: "I do believe, Lord: help my unbelief."[11]

This Lack of Confidence Is Very Harmful to Them

Lack of confidence, whatever be its cause, does us much harm and deprives us of great blessings.

When Saint Peter, in his eager desire to meet Our Lord, jumped from his boat into the lake, he walked upon the waters with an assured step. But the wind blew violently. Soon the waves rose angrily, threatening to engulf him. Peter trembled with fear. He hesitated . . .and began to sink. "O thou of little faith," Jesus said to him, "why didst thou doubt?"[12]

And so it is with us. In our moments of fervor, we remain tranquil and recollected at the feet of Our Lord. When the tempest comes, the danger engrosses our attention. We turn our eyes away from Our Lord to fix them anxiously on our trials and our dangers. We hesitate. . . and then we sink.

Temptation assails us. Our duties seem tiresome and disagreeable. Disturbing thoughts take possession of us. The storm rages in our intellect, in our sensibility, and in our flesh. Passion overcomes us; we fall into sin; we give way to a discouragement more pernicious than the sin itself. Souls without confidence, why do we doubt?

Trials come to us in a thousand forms. Our temporal affairs are in a dangerous state; we worry about the future. People slander us, and our reputation is injured. Death breaks the ties of our deepest, most tender affections. We forget then the fatherly care that Providence has for us. We murmur, we rebel; thus we increase our difficulties and the bitterness of our suffering. Souls without confidence, why do we doubt?

If we had clung to Our Lord with a confidence that grew in proportion to the apparent desperation of our situation, we would have suffered no harm. We would have walked safely and calmly on the waves; we would have reached the tranquil and safe gulf without accident. Soon we would have found ourselves on the sunny shore that is illuminated by the light of heaven.

The saints struggled against the same difficulties; some of them committed the same faults. But at least they never lost confidence. More humble after their fall, they rose without delay, relying henceforth only on God's assistance. They preserved in their hearts the absolute certainty that, trusting in God, they could do all things. And their hope did not confound them.[13] Begin, then, to be confident souls. Our Lord exhorts you to this. Your interests demand it. And, at the same time, your souls will have light and peace.

Goal and Content of This Book

This work has no other end than to incite you to the knowledge and practice of the virtue of confidence. Accordingly, its nature, objects, foundation, and effects will be expounded here very simply. O pious reader, if this modest little book should sometime fall into your hands, do not put it aside. It does not pretend to literary distinction or originality. It merely contains consoling truths that I have collected from the Scriptures and the writings of the saints. And this is its unique merit.

Try to read it slowly, with attention, in a spirit of prayer. I would almost say: Meditate on it! Allow the teachings in its pages to sink deeply into your soul; they contain the quintessence of the Gospel. Could there be a better food for souls than the words of Our Lord?

May you, upon finishing this reading, be able to confide solely in the Divine Master Who has given us everything: the treasures of His Heart, His love, His life, to the very last drop of His Blood!

CHAPTER TWO
Nature and Characteristics of Confidence

"The Lord is my light and my salvation, whom shall I fear? The Lord is the protector of my life: Of whom shall I be afraid?"

—Psalms 26:1

"Confidence is a hope fortified by solid conviction."
—Saint Thomas Aquinas, Doctor of the Church

NATURE AND CHARACTERISTICS OF CONFIDENCE

Confidence Is a Firm Hope

With words that bear the mark of his genius, Saint Thomas Aquinas defines confidence with this conciseness that bears the mark of his genius as "a hope fortified by solid conviction."[1] We will devote this chapter to the explanation of these profound words.

Let us attentively consider the terms employed by the Angelic Doctor.

"Confidence," he writes, "is a hope." It is not that ordinary hope common to all the faithful; a precise qualifier distinguishes it: it is "a fortified hope."

However, note well, there is no difference in nature, only in degree. The faint glimmer of the dawn and the dazzling light of the sun at its zenith form part of the same day. So hope and confidence pertain to the same virtue; one is the complete blossoming of the other.

Ordinary hope is lost by despair. It can tolerate, however, a certain amount of anxiety. But, when it reaches that perfection which merits for it the name of Confidence, then it becomes more delicate and more sensitive.

It can no longer bear hesitation, however insignificant it may be; the slightest doubt would lessen it and so reduce it to the level of mere hope.

The Royal Prophet David selects his words most precisely when he calls confidence "a super hope."[2] It is, indeed, a question of a virtue carried to the very highest degree attainable. And Father Saint-Jure, one of the most esteemed spiritual writers of the seventeenth century, justly terms it an "extraordinary and heroic hope."[3]

Confidence is not, then, a common flower. It grows on the crests; it does not permit itself to be picked except by magnanimous souls.

Confidence Is Fortified by Faith

Let us take this study further.

What sovereign strength fortifies hope to the point of rendering it unshakable in the face of the assault of adversity? Faith!

The confident soul remains mindful of the promises of her Heavenly Father; she meditates upon them profoundly. She knows that God's word cannot fail, and from this she draws her certainty. Danger may threaten, surround, and even strike her, but she always preserves her serenity. In spite of the imminent danger, she repeats the words of the Psalmist: "The Lord is my light and my salvation, whom shall I fear? The Lord is the protector of my life: Of whom shall I be afraid?"[4]

There is the closest affinity between faith and confidence; the two are most intimately related. A contemporary theologian tells us that confidence has its "source and root"[5] in faith. Hence the more profound our faith, the stronger and more deeply rooted will be our confidence. In the Scriptures, we find that the sacred writers designated these two virtues by the same word: *fides.*

Confidence Is Unshakable

The preceding considerations may appear to be excessively abstract. It was necessary for us, however, to establish our foundation upon these considerations. From them we shall deduce the characteristics of true confidence.

"Confidence," writes Father Saint-Jure, "is firm, stable, and constant to such an eminent degree that it cannot be shaken—I no longer say just overthrown—by anything in the world."[6]

Neither the most afflicting temporal misfortunes nor the greatest spiritual difficulties will disturb the peace of the confident soul. Unforeseen calamities may lay her happiness in ruins around her; this soul, more master of herself than the ancient wise man, will remain calm: "*Impavidum ferient ruinae.*"[7]

She will simply turn to the Lord. She will lean on Him with a certainty that increases in proportion to the degree that she feels herself deprived of human help. She will pray with greater fervor and, in the darkness of the trial, continue on her path, waiting in silence for the hour of God.

Such confidence, no doubt, is rare. But, unless it attains this minimum of perfection, it does not merit the name of confidence.

We find sublime examples of this degree of confidence in the Scriptures and in the lives of the saints.

Such was the confidence of Job. Stricken with every possible misfortune—the loss of his wealth, the death of his children, the ruin of his health—he was reduced to direst poverty and afflicted with a dreadful disease. As he sat on a dunghill, his friends, even his wife, increased his pain by the cruelty of their words. But he did not allow himself to be discouraged; no murmuring was mixed with his groaning. He kept his mind fixed on thoughts of faith. "Although He [the Lord] should kill me," he said, "I will trust in Him."[8]

This was an admirable confidence that God rewarded

magnificently. The trial ceased; Job recovered his health, gained a considerable fortune again, and enjoyed a life more prosperous than the one he had before the trial.

On one of his journeys, Saint Martin fell into the hands of highwaymen.

The bandits stripped him and were going to kill him. Suddenly, however, touched by the grace of repentance or moved by a mysterious fear, they turned him loose and, against all expectations, freed him. Later, the illustrious bishop was asked if, during that pressing danger, he had not felt some fear.

"None," he responded. "I knew that as human help became more improbable, the divine intervention was all the more certain."

Unfortunately, most Christians do not imitate such examples.

Never do they approach God so seldom as in the hour of trial. Indeed, many do not even send forth that cry for help which God awaits in order to come to their assistance. What a fatal negligence! "Providence," Louis of Granada used to say, "wishes to give the solution to the extraordinary difficulties of life directly, while it leaves to secondary causes the resolving of ordinary difficulties."[9] But it is always necessary to cry out for divine help.

That help God gives us with pleasure. "Far from bothering the nurse who suckles him, the baby brings her relief."[10]

Other Christians pray fervently, but they do not persevere in prayer. If they are not answered immediately, they quickly fall from exalted hope into a state of unreasonable discouragement. They do not understand the ways of grace. God treats us like children; He plays deaf at times because He likes to hear us invoking Him. Why should we become discouraged so quickly when, on the contrary, it would be convenient for us to cry out with greater insistence?

This is the doctrine taught by Saint Francis de Sales: "Providence only delays in coming to our aid in order to excite us to confidence. If our Heavenly Father does not always grant us what we ask, it is because He desires to keep us at His feet and to provide us with an occasion to insist with loving violence in our petitions to Him. He showed this clearly to the two disciples at Emmaus, with whom He did not consent to remain until the close of the day, and even after they had pressed Him."[11]

Confidence Counts on Nothing but God

Unshakable firmness is, then, the first characteristic of confidence.

The second quality of this virtue is even more perfect. It leads a man not to count on the help of creatures, whether such help be drawn from himself, from his own intelligence, from his judgment, from his knowledge, from his skill, from his riches, from his friends, from his relatives, or from any other thing of his; or whether it be assistance that he might perhaps hope to receive from someone else: kings, princes, or any creature in general, because he senses and knows the weaknesses of all human help. He considers human helps to be what they really are. How right Saint Teresa was in calling them "dry branches that break under the first pressure."[12]

But, some will say, does not this theory proceed from false mysticism? Will it not lead to fatalism or, at least, to perilous passivity? Why should we multiply our efforts in trying to overcome difficulties if all human support must crumble in our hands? Let us simply cross our arms and await divine intervention!

No, God does not wish us to sleep; He demands that we imitate Him. His perfect activity has no limits. He is pure act.

We must act, then, but from Him alone must we expect the efficacy of our action. "Help thyself that heaven may help thee." Behold the economy of the providential plan.

To your posts then! Let us work with our spirit and heart turned on high. "It is vain for you to rise before light,"[13] says the Scripture; if the Lord does not aid thee, thou shalt attain nothing.

Indeed, our impotence is radical. "Without Me you can do nothing," says Our Savior.[14] In the supernatural order, this impotence is absolute. Heed well the teachings of the theologians.

Without grace, man cannot observe the commandments of God for a long time or in their totality. Without grace, he cannot resist all the temptations, sometimes so violent, that assault him.

Without grace, we cannot have a good thought; we cannot even make the shortest prayer; without it, we cannot even invoke with piety the holy name of Jesus.

Everything that we do in the supernatural order comes to us from God alone.[15] Even in the natural order, it is still God who gives us victory.

Saint Peter had worked the whole night; he had endured in his labors; he had a profound knowledge of the secrets of his difficult occupation. Nevertheless, his movements over the gentle waves of the lake had been in vain; he had caught nothing. Then he receives the Master into his boat; upon casting his net in the name of the Savior, he attains an undeniably miraculous catch; the nets break, such is the number of fish.

Following the example of the Apostle, let us cast our nets with untiring patience; but let us hope only in Our Lord for the miraculous catch.

Saint Ignatius of Loyola used to say: "In everything you do, behold the rule of rules to follow: Trust in God, acting, nevertheless, as if success in everything depended entirely on you and not at all on God; but, employing your efforts to attain this good result, do not count on them, but proceed as if everything were done by God alone and nothing by you."[16]

Confidence Rejoices Even at Being Deprived of Human Help

Do not be discouraged when the mirage of human assistance fades away. To count on nothing but the help of heaven, is this not already a most high virtue?

Even so, the vigorous wings of true confidence rise to even more sublime regions. It reaches them by a kind of refinement of heroism. Then it attains the highest degree of its perfection. This degree consists in the soul rejoicing when it finds itself stripped of all human support, abandoned by its relatives, its friends, and all the creatures who do not wish to or cannot help it, who cannot give it counsel or assist it with their talents or credits, who have no means left to come to its aid.[17]

What a profound wisdom this joy denotes in such cruel circumstances!

To intone the Canticle of Alleluia under blows which are, naturally speaking, sufficient to break our courage, one must know the Heart of Our Lord to Its depth; one must believe blindly in His merciful and fatherly love and His omnipotent goodness; one must have absolute certainty that He selects for His intervention the hour of the desperate situations.

After his conversion, Saint Francis of Assisi despised the dreams of glory that had dazzled him previously. He fled from human gatherings, withdrew into the forest in order to surrender himself to a long period of prayer, and gave generous alms. This change displeased his father, who, dragging his son before the diocesan authority, accused him of dissipating his goods. Then, in the presence of the marveling bishop, Francis renounced his paternal inheritance, removed the clothing that had come to him from his family, and stripped himself of everything! Then, vibrant with supernatural happiness, he exclaimed: "Now, yes, O my God, I can call Thee more truly than ever, 'Our Father, Who art in heaven'!" Behold how the saints act.

You souls wounded by misfortune, do not murmur over the abandonment in which you find yourselves reduced. God does not ask of you a sensible joy, impossible to your weakness. Just rekindle your faith, have courage, and, according to the expression dear to Saint Francis de Sales, in the "innermost point of your soul," try to have joy.

Providence will eventually give you the right sign by which you shall recognize Its hour; It deprived you of all support. Now is the moment to resist the distress of nature. You have reached that hour in the office of the interior of the soul in which you should sing the Magnificat and put incense to burn. "Rejoice in the Lord always; again, I say, rejoice... The Lord is nigh!"[18] Follow this counsel, you will feel the benefit of it.

If the Divine Master did not allow Himself to be touched by such confidence, He would not be the same Person shown by the Gospel to be so compassionate, the One who trembled with painful emotion at the sight of our suffering.

Our Lord once said to a saintly religious, who died in the

odor of sanctity: "If I am good to all, I am very good to those who confide in Me. Dost thou know which souls take the greatest advantage of my goodness? They are those who hope the most. Confident souls steal my graces!"[19]

CHAPTER THREE

Confidence in God and Our Temporal Necessities

---

*"Seek ye, therefore, first the kingdom of
God and His justice, and all these things
shall be added unto you."*
—Matt. 6:33

"Consider the lilies of the field, how they grow: they labor not, neither do they spin. But I say to you that not even Solomon in all his glory was arrayed as one of these. And if the grass of the field, which is today, and tomorrow is cast into the oven, God doth so clothe: how much more you, O ye of little faith?"
—Matt. 6:28-30

CONFIDENCE IN GOD AND OUR TEMPORAL NECESSITIES

God Provides for Our Temporal Necessities

Confidence, we have already said, is a heroic hope; it does not differ from the common hope of all the faithful except in its degree of perfection. It is, then, exercised upon the same objects as that virtue but by means of acts that are more intense and vibrant.

Like ordinary hope, confidence expects from our heavenly Father all the aids necessary for living a holy life here on earth and for meriting the happiness of Paradise. It expects, first of all, temporal goods, to the degree that these can lead us to our final end.

There is nothing more logical. We cannot proceed to conquer heaven as pure spirits; we are composed of body and soul. The body that the Creator formed with His adorable hands is our inseparable companion in our terrestrial existence, and it will also be the partaker of our eternal fortune after the general resurrection. We cannot act without its assistance in the battle for the conquest of our blessed life.

Now, then, in order to maintain itself and to fulfill its task completely, the body has multiple demands. It is necessary that Providence satisfy these demands, and it does so magnificently.

God takes upon Himself the responsibility of providing for our necessities, and this He does generously. He follows us with a vigilant eye and does not leave us in need. Amidst material difficulties, even anguishing ones, we must not become disturbed. With complete certainty we must hope to receive from the Divine Hands that which is necessary to maintain our lives.

"Therefore I say to you," declares the Savior, "be not solicitous for your life, what you shall eat, nor for your body, what you shall put on. Is not the life more than the meat, and the body more than the raiment?

"Behold the birds of the air, for they neither sow, nor do they reap, nor gather into barns: and your heavenly Father feedeth them. Are not you of much more value than they? . . .And for raiment why are you solicitous?

"Consider the lilies of the field, how they grow: they labor not, neither do they spin. But I say to you, that not even Solomon in all his glory was arrayed as one of these. And if the grass of the field, which is today, and tomorrow is cast into the oven, God doth so clothe: how much more you, O ye of little faith?

"Be not solicitous therefore, saying 'What shall we eat, or what shall we drink, or wherewith shall we be clothed?' For after all these things do the heathens seek. For your Father knoweth that you have need of all these things.

"Seek ye therefore first the kingdom of God, and His justice, and all these things shall be added unto you."[1]

It is not enough for us to skip lightly over this discourse of Our Lord. We must fix our attention on it for a long time in order to seek its profound significance and to imbue our souls deeply with its doctrine.

God Provides According to the Situation of Each One

Should we take these words literally and understand them in their most restricted sense? Will God give us only that which is strictly necessary: a piece of dry bread, a glass of water, a bit of cloth that our misery urgently requires? No, the heavenly Father does not treat His sons with avaricious frugality. To think thus would be to blaspheme against the Divine Goodness, and, if I may say so, to be ignorant of His ways. In the exercise of His providence, as well as in His created works, God indeed employs great prodigality.

When He spread the world out through space, He drew thousands of stars out of nothing. In the Milky Way, that immense region of luminous nights, is not every grain of sand a world?

When He feeds the birds, He invites them to the most opulent table of nature. He offers them the ear-filled corn, the grains of all kinds that mature on the plants, the fruits from the autumn woods, the seeds that the farmers scatter in the furrows. What a varied list going on to infinity for the nourishment of these humble little creatures!

When He created vegetation, with what grace did He decorate its flowers! He made a crown for them inlaid with precious jewels; He put fragrant perfumes in their chalices; He spun their petals of silk, so brilliant and delicate that the artifices of industry will never equal their beauty.

And, then, when it is a question of man, His masterpiece, the adoptive brother of the Word Incarnate, would not God show Himself to be even more generous?

Let us consider, then, as an indisputable truth, that Providence does provide abundantly for the temporal necessities of man.

Unquestionably, there will always be rich and poor on the earth. While some live in abundance, others must work and practice a wholesome economy. The heavenly Father, however, furnishes all with the means to live with a certain well-being according to the conditions in which He has placed them.

Let us return to the comparison that Jesus employs. God vested the lily splendidly with that white and perfumed garment required by its nature.

The violet was dressed more modestly; God gave it,

however, that which fits its particular nature. And these two flowers blossom sweetly in the sun, lacking nothing that is necessary to them.

And so God acts with men. He puts some of them in the higher classes of society; and others He puts in less brilliant conditions; but to the one and to the other He nevertheless gives what is necessary for maintaining their positions in a dignified way.

An objection arises here in respect to the instability of social conditions. In the present crisis, is it not easier to fall than to rise or even to maintain oneself at the same social level?

Without a doubt. But Divine Providence distributes exactly the aid necessary for each one. For great evils He sends great remedies. That which economic catastrophes take from us, we can reacquire through our industry and our work. In those very rare cases in which our activity is rendered impossible, we have the right to hope for exceptional intervention from God.

Generally (at least this is the way I think), God does not bring about *falls*. He desires, on the contrary, that we develop ourselves, that we rise, that we grow with prudence. If, at times, He permits a decline in our social level, He does not wish this except as a manifestation of a posterior will, a will posterior to the action of our free will. More often than not, such a decline results from our own fault, either personal or hereditary. It is commonly a natural consequence of laziness, prodigality, or of various passions.

And even though a man has fallen, he can raise himself back up and, with the help of Providence, regain by his efforts the situation that he has lost.

We Must Not Trouble Ourselves about the Future

God provides for our necessities.

"Be not solicitous," says Our Lord.

What is the exact sense of this counsel? In order to obey the directions of the Master, must we completely neglect our temporal affairs?

We do not doubt that, at times, grace asks from certain souls the sacrifice required by strict poverty and total abandonment to Providence.

Nevertheless, the rarity of these vocations is notable. The others, be they religious communities or individuals, have goods; they must manage them prudently.

The Holy Ghost praises the strong woman who knows how to govern her house well. In the Book of Proverbs, He shows her to us rising very early to distribute to her servants their daily tasks and working with her own hands as well. Nothing escapes her watchfulness. The members of her household have nothing to fear. Thanks to her foresight, they shall have what is necessary, agreeable, and even, to a certain extent, moderately luxurious. Her children proclaim her blessed, and her husband exalts her virtues.[2]

The Truth would not have praised that woman so warmly if she had not fulfilled her obligations.

It behooves us, then, not to afflict ourselves. We must occupy ourselves reasonably with our obligations, not allowing ourselves to be dominated by anguish over the somber prospects of the future, and counting without hesitation on the aid of Divine Providence.

Have no illusions! Such confidence demands great strength of soul. We have to avoid a double shoal: an excess and a deficiency. On the one hand, he who, from negligence, takes no interest in his obligations and affairs cannot hope for extraordinary help from God without tempting Him. On the other hand, he who gives his material concerns the first place in his thoughts, who counts more upon himself than upon God, deceives himself even more crassly; he robs the Most High of the place in his life that belongs to Him.

"In medio stat virtus": Between these two extremes duty is found.

If we have taken prudent care of our interests, to be afflicted about the future would amount to ignoring and despising the power and the goodness of God.

During the long years Saint Paul the Hermit lived in the desert, a crow brought him a half loaf of bread every day. One day Saint Anthony came to visit the illustrious solitary. The two saints conversed for a long time, forgetting during their pious meditations the necessity for food. But Providence thought of them: The crow came, this time carrying a whole loaf.

The heavenly Father created the whole universe with one single word; can it be difficult for Him to assist His sons in their hour of need? Saint Camillus of Lellis went into debt in order to help the sick poor. Seeing this, his fellow religious became alarmed. "Why doubt Providence?" the Saint quieted them. "Can it be difficult for Our Lord to give us a little of those goods that He heaps upon the Jews and the Turks, enemies one and the other of our Faith?"[3] The confidence of Camillus was not disappointed; one month later, one of his protectors, upon dying, left him a considerable sum.

To be afflicted about the future constitutes a lack of confidence that offends God and provokes His anger.

When the Hebrews became lost in the sands of the desert after their flight from Egypt, they forgot the miracles that the Lord had worked in their favor. They were afraid and murmured: "Can God furnish a table in the wilderness?... Can He also give bread, or provide a table for His people?" These words angered the Lord. He hurled down fire from heaven upon them; His wrath fell over Israel, "because they believed not in God:

and trusted not in His salvation."[4]

There is no need to be afflicted; the Father watches over us.

Seeking First the Kingdom of God and His Justice

"Seek ye therefore first the Kingdom of God, and His justice, and all these things shall be added unto you."

It was thus that the Savior concluded the discourse on Providence. A consoling conclusion, it includes a conditional promise; it depends on us to be benefited by it. The Lord will occupy Himself all the more with our interests when we concern ourselves with His interests.

It behooves us to stop and meditate on the words of the Master.

A question immediately arises: Where is the kingdom of God, which we must seek before all else?

"Within you," the Gospel answers. "*Regnum Dei intra vos est.*"[5]

To seek the kingdom of God is, then, to erect a throne for Him in our souls, to submit ourselves entirely to His sovereign dominion. Let us keep all of our faculties under the merciful scepter of the Most High. Let our intelligence be mindful of His constant presence; let our will conform itself in everything with His adorable will; let our hearts fly to Him frequently in acts of ardent and sincere charity. Then we shall have practiced that "justice" which, in the words of the Scriptures, signifies the perfection of the interior life.

We shall have followed to the letter the counsel of the Master; we shall have sought the kingdom of God.

"And all these things shall be added unto you."

There is, here, a kind of bilateral contract: On our part we work for the glory of the heavenly Father; on His part, the Father commits Himself to provide for our necessities.

"Cast thy care upon the Lord." Fulfill the contract that He proposes to you; He will fulfill the given word. He will watch over you, and "He will sustain you."[6]

"Think of Me," said the Savior to Saint Catherine of Siena, "and I will think of thee." And, centuries later, in the convent of Paray, He promised Saint Margaret Mary that those particularly devoted to the Sacred Heart would have success in their undertakings.

Happy the Christian who conforms well to this maxim of the Gospel! He seeks God, and God looks after his interests with His omnipotence; what can be lacking to him? "The Lord ruleth me: and I shall want nothing."[7]

Practice the solid interior virtues, and thus avoid all disorder: the faults and vices that are the most common causes of failure and ruin.

Praying for Our Temporal Necessities

Confidence, as we have just been describing it, does not take away from us the obligation of prayer. In our temporal necessities, it is not enough for us to await the assistance of God; we must also ask Him for it.

Jesus Christ left us the perfect model of prayer. Therein He makes us ask for our "daily bread": "Give us this day our daily bread."

In regard to this obligation of prayer, is there not possibly frequent negligence on our part? What imprudence and what foolishness! We deprive ourselves, out of levity, of the protection of God, the only supremely efficacious one.

The Capuchins, the legend says, never die of hunger because they always piously recite the Our Father. Let us imitate them, and the Most High will not leave us wanting in our necessities. Let us ask, then, for our daily bread. It is an obligation imposed on us by faith and by charity to ourselves.

Can we raise our pretensions, however, and also ask for riches? Nothing is opposed to this, as long as this plea is inspired by supernatural motives and we stay fully submissive to the will of God. The Lord does not prohibit the expression of our desires; on the contrary, He wishes us to be quite open with Him. Let us not expect, however, that He bend to our fantasies; the very Divine Goodness itself is opposed to this. God knows what is good for us. And He will concede to us the goods of the earth only if they can serve for our sanctification.

Let us hand ourselves over completely to the direction of Providence, saying the prayer of the wise man: "Remove far from me vanity, and lying words. Give me neither beggary, nor riches: give me only the necessaries of life. Lest perhaps being filled, I should be tempted to deny, and say: 'Who is the Lord?' or being compelled by poverty, I should steal, and forswear the name of my God."[8]

CHAPTER FOUR
Confidence in God and Our Spiritual Necessities

"Guilty souls, do not fear the Savior; it was especially for you that He came down to earth."

"Behold the birds of the air, for they neither sow, nor do they reap, nor gather into barns: and your heavenly Father feedeth them. Are not you of much more value than they?"

—Matt. 6:26

CONFIDENCE IN GOD AND OUR SPIRITUAL NECESSITIES

Our Lord Is Merciful to Sinners

Divine Providence feeds the birds of the trees; It also takes care of our bodies. What is this body of misery? A fragile creature, one condemned to death and destined to be consumed by worms.

In the mad rush of life, we think that all things lead to business or to pleasures. However, every step moves us closer to the end. We ourselves drag our corpses to the edge of the grave.

If God so concerns Himself with perishable bodies, with what solicitude will He not look after our immortal souls? He prepares for them treasures of grace, whose riches exceed all that we can imagine. He sends them superabundant help for their sanctification and salvation.

These means of sanctification that the Faith puts at our disposal will not be studied here.

I merely wish to speak to the worried souls that one finds everywhere. With the Gospel in my hand, I will show them the emptiness of their fears.

Neither the gravity of their faults nor their multiple relapses into errors should overwhelm them.

On the contrary, the more they sense the weight of their own misery, the more they should lean upon God. Let them not lose confidence! However horrible their state may be, even though they may have led a disorderly life for a long time, with the help of grace, they can convert and be raised to high perfection.

The mercy of Our Lord is infinite; nothing exhausts it, not even faults that appear to us to be the most degrading and criminal ones. During His mortal life the Master received sinners with a truly divine goodness; He never refused them pardon.

Moved by the ardor of her repentance, Mary Magdalen enters the banquet hall. Without worrying about worldly conventions, she prostrates herself before the feet of Jesus, inundating them with tears. Simon, the Pharisee, contemplates the scene with a sarcastic air; he becomes indignant within himself. "If this man were a prophet," he thinks, "he would know surely what this woman is worth. He would reject her with disdain." But the Savior does not reject her. He accepts her sighs, her tears, all the sensible signs of her humble contrition. He purifies her of her stains and showers her with supernatural gifts. And His Sacred Heart overflows with immense joy, while on high, in the Kingdom of His Father, the angels vibrate with jubilation and praise. A soul that was lost has been found; a soul was dead, and, behold, it is again restored to true life!

The Master is not content with receiving poor sinners with sweetness; He goes so far as to take up their defense. And is this not, furthermore, His mission? Did He not make Himself *our advocate*?[1]

One day they bring him a wretched woman, surprised in the flagrant act of her sin. The harsh law of Moses condemns her formally; the guilty person must die the slow torment of stoning.

Nevertheless, the Scribes and Pharisees wait impatiently for the sentence of the Savior. If He pardons her, His enemies will accuse Him for despising the traditions of Israel. What will He do?

A single word will fall from His lips, and this word will be enough to confound the proud Pharisees and save the sinful woman.

"He that is without sin among you, let him first cast a stone at her."[2]

An answer full of wisdom and of mercy. Hearing it, these arrogant men blush with shame. They withdraw, confounded, one after the other; the ancients are the first to flee.

And Jesus is left alone with the woman. "Where are they that accused thee?" He asks. "Hath no man condemned thee?"

She answers: "No man, Lord." And Jesus continues: "Neither will I condemn thee! Go, and now sin no more!"[3]

When sinners come to Him, Jesus hurries to meet them. Like the father of the prodigal son, He is waiting for the return of the ungrateful ones. Like the good shepherd, He seeks after the lost sheep; and when He finds it, He puts it on His divine shoulders and restores it bloodstained to the fold.

Oh! He will not irritate its wounds; like the good Samaritan, He will treat them with symbolic wine and oil. Over its sores, He will pour the balsam of penitence; and, in order to fortify it, He will make it drink of His Eucharistic chalice.

Guilty souls, do not fear the Savior; it was especially for you that He came down to earth. Never renew the cry of despair of Cain: "My iniquity is greater than that I may deserve pardon."[4] How this would amount to being ignorant of the Heart of Jesus!

Jesus purified Magdalen and pardoned the triple denial of Peter. He opened heaven to the good thief. In truth, I assure you, if Judas had gone to Him after the crime, Our Lord would have received him with mercy.

How, then, would He not pardon you as well?

Grace Can Sanctify Us in an Instant

Abyss of human weakness, tyranny of bad habits! How many Christians receive in the tribunal of Penance absolution for their sins. Their contrition is sincere, they make vigorous resolutions... and they fall again into the same sins, sometimes grave; the number of their falls grows without ceasing! Do they not have, then, abundant reason for discouragement?

Nothing is more just than that the evidence of our own misery keeps us humble. That it should make us lose confidence would be a catastrophe more dangerous than so many falls into error.

The soul that falls should rise immediately. It should not cease to implore the mercy of the Lord. Do you not know that God has *His hours* and can, in an instant, elevate us to a very high degree of sanctity?

Had not Mary Magdalen led a criminal life? Grace, nevertheless, transformed her instantaneously. Without transition, a sinner became a great saint. Now, then, the action of God has not been reduced in what it can do.

What it did for others it will be able to do for us. Do not doubt. Confident and persevering prayer will obtain a complete cure of our souls.

Do not tell me that time passes and that now, perhaps, your life is reaching its end.

Our Lord waited for the agony of the good thief in order to attract him victoriously to Himself. In one single minute, that man of such guilt converted! His faith and his love were so great that, in spite of his great crimes, he did not even pass through purgatory. He occupies an elevated place in heaven forever.

Let nothing, then, alter your confidence! Even though you be in the depths of the abyss, call out to heaven without ceasing. God will end by responding to your cry and will work His justice in you.

God Grants Us All the Necessary Helps for the Sanctification and Salvation of Our Souls

Certain anguished souls doubt their own salvation. They dwell too much on their past faults; they think of the violent temptations that at times assault all of us; they forget the merciful goodness of God. This anguish can become a veritable temptation to despair.

While a young man, Saint Francis de Sales experienced a trial of this kind. He trembled at the thought of not being predestined to heaven and passed through a number of months in this interior martyrdom. A heroic prayer freed him: the Saint prostrated himself before an altar of Mary, beseeching the Virgin to teach him to love her Son with a charity as ardent on earth as the fear he had of not being able to love Him in eternity.

In this form of suffering, there is a truth of faith that should console us immensely. We are lost only by *mortal sin.*

This we can always avoid, and, even when we have suffered the disgrace of committing it, we can always be reconciled with God. An act of sincere contrition, made immediately, without postponement, will purify us, while we await the obligatory confession, which should be made without delay.

Certainly the poor human will should always distrust its weakness. But the Savior will never refuse us the graces that we lack. He will also do everything possible to help us in the supremely important endeavor to save our souls.

Behold the great truth that Jesus Christ wrote with His precious Blood and that we are now going to reread together in the history of His Passion.

Have you ever reflected upon how the Jews were able to seize Our Lord? Do you believe, perhaps, that they succeeded in this crime by cunning or by force? Is it possible to think that, amid the great turmoil, Jesus was overcome because He was the weaker?

Certainly not. His enemies could do nothing against Him. In the three years of His preaching, they wanted to throw Him from a cliff; on various occasions they took up rocks to stone Him. Always, however, the Divine Word frustrated the plans of the impious; the sovereign force of God held back their hands, and Jesus always calmly withdrew, without anyone having been able to do Him the slightest harm.

In Gethsemane, the soldiers of the Temple came to take possession of His sacred person. Upon His merely uttering His name, the whole band of soldiers fell to the ground, gripped by a strange fear. The soldiers could rise only after being given permission by Him.

If Jesus was taken prisoner, if He was crucified, if He was immolated, it was because He so wanted it, in the plenitude of His liberty and His love for us. "He was offered because it was His own will."[5]

If the Master unhesitatingly shed His precious Blood wholly for us, if He died for us, how could He refuse us the graces that are absolutely necessary for us and that He Himself merited for us by His sufferings?

During His Passion, Jesus mercifully offered these graces to the most guilty souls. Two Apostles had committed enormous crimes; to both He offered pardon. Judas betrayed Him with a hypocritical kiss. Jesus spoke to him with a touching gentleness; He called him *His friend*. By tender affection He sought to touch that heart hardened by avarice. "Friend, whereto art thou come?" "Judas, dost thou betray the Son of Man with a kiss?"[6] This is the last grace of the Master to the ungrateful one.

It is a grace of such force that we will never be able to measure adequately its intensity. Judas, however, rejects it; he is lost, because he formally prefers that state.

Peter believes himself to be very strong. He had sworn to accompany the Master till death, but he abandons Him when he sees Him in the hands of the soldiers. Thereafter, he follows Him only from a distance. He enters trembling into the courtyard of the palace of the High Priest.

Three times he denies his Lord—because he fears the derision of a maidservant. With an oath he affirms that he does not know "that man." The cock crows... Jesus turns and fixes his eyes on the Apostle, eyes filled with merciful and gentle censures. Their gazes meet.

It is a grace, a fulminating grace, that is carried to Peter by that gaze. The Apostle does not reject it; he goes out and weeps bitterly over his faults.

As in the case of Judas and Peter, Jesus always offers us graces of repentance and conversion. We can accept or refuse them. We are free! It is for us to decide between good and evil, between heaven and hell. Salvation is in our hands. The Savior not only offers us His graces, He does more: He intercedes for us before the heavenly Father. He reminds Him of the pains suffered for our Redemption. He takes up our defense before Him; He excuses our faults.

"Father," He exclaims in the anguish of the agony, "forgive them, for they know not what they do."[7] During the Passion, the Master had such a desire to save us that He did not cease for an instant to think of us.

On Calvary, He gives His last gaze to sinners; He pronounces one of His last words in favor of the good thief. He extends His arms wide on the Cross in order to indicate with what love He receives each repentant soul in His most loving Heart.

The Sight of the Crucifix Should Revive Our Confidence

If ever in your intimate struggles you feel yourself weakening in confidence, meditate on the passages of the Gospel that I have just pointed out to you.

Contemplate that ignominious cross upon which your God expired. Look at His poor head crowned with thorns, falling inert upon His breast. Consider those candid eyes and the pale countenance whereon the precious blood coagulates. Look at the pierced feet and hands and at the mortally wounded body. Pay attention, above all, to the most loving Heart that was opened by the soldier's lance; from it flows a few drops of bloodstained water. All this He gave you! How is it possible to distrust this Savior?

From you, however, He expects the gratitude of affection. In the name of His love, in the name of His martyrdom, in the name of His death, make the resolution to avoid mortal sin in the future.

Weakness is great, I well know, but He will help you. In spite of having goodwill, you will perhaps have falls and relapses into evil, but the Lord is merciful. He only asks that you not let yourself fall asleep in sin, that you fight against bad habits.

Promise Him to confess promptly and never to pass through a night with a mortal sin on your conscience. If you keep this resolution courageously, you will be happy. Jesus will not have shed His precious Blood for you in vain.

Be calm regarding your intimate dispositions. In this way, you will have the right to serenely face the fearful problem of predestination. You will carry on your forehead the sign of the elect.

CHAPTER FIVE
Reasons for Confidence in God

---

*"He will wipe away our tears for all eternity.
Then there will be no more weeping, nor
want, nor mourning, for He will have ended
the era of our misery."*

The Finding in the Temple, Church of the Sacred Heart of Jesus, São Paulo, Brazil.

"For a Child is born to us, and a son is given to us, and the government is upon his shoulder: and his name shall be called, Wonderful, Counsellor, God the Mighty, the Father of the world to come, the Prince of Peace."
—Isaias 9:6

REASONS FOR CONFIDENCE IN GOD

The Incarnation of the Word

The wise man builds his house upon a rock. Neither floods, nor rains, nor tempests can destroy it. In order for the edifice of our confidence to resist all tests, it must be built on an unshakable foundation.

"Do you wish to know," asked Saint Francis de Sales, "what foundation our confidence must have? It must be based on the infinite goodness of God and the merits of the Passion and Death of Our Lord Jesus Christ, with this condition on our part: a firm and total resolution to belong wholly to God and to abandon ourselves entirely and without reservation to His Providence."[1]

The reasons for hope are too numerous for us to be able to cite them all. We shall examine here only those that are furnished to us by the Incarnation of the Word and by the Sacred Person of Our Savior. Moreover, Christ is, in truth, the "cornerstone"[2] upon which our interior life must principally rest.

With what confidence the mystery of the Incarnation would inspire us if we made an effort to study it in a less superficial manner!

Who is that infant who weeps in the manger, that child who works in the shop at Nazareth, that preacher who inspires the multitudes, that wonderworker who performs countless prodigies, that innocent victim who dies on the Cross?

He is the Son of the Most High, the eternal God as is the Father. He is the Emmanuel who has so long been hoped for. It is He whom the prophet calls "Wonderful, Counselor, God the

Mighty... the Prince of Peace."[3]

But Jesus—we forget this frequently—is our property. In all the rigor of the term, He belongs to us; He is ours, and we have inalienable rights over Him, for the heavenly Father gave Him to us. The Scripture affirms it thus: "For a child is born to us, and a son is given to us."[4]

And Saint John in his Gospel also says: "For God so loved the world, as to give His only-begotten Son."[5]

Now, then, if Christ belongs to us, the infinite merits of His works, of His sufferings, and of His death also belong to us. This being the case, how can we lose our courage? By giving us His Son, the Father of heaven gave us the Plenitude of all goods. Let us know how to explore thoroughly this precious treasure.

Let us, then, offer up our prayers to heaven with holy audacity, and, in the name of the Redeemer who is ours, let us without hesitation implore all the graces that we desire. Let us ask for temporal blessings and, above all, for the help of grace. Let us ask for peace and prosperity for our country, and tranquility and liberty for the Church. This prayer will certainly be attended.

In acting this way, do we not make a bargain with God? In exchange for the desired goods, we offer Him His only Son. And in this transaction, God cannot be defrauded; we give Him infinitely more than we can receive from Him.

If we make this prayer with the faith that moves mountains, it will be sufficiently effective to obtain—if they be necessary—even the most extraordinary prodigies.

The Power of Our Lord

The Incarnate Word, who gave Himself to us, possesses an unlimited power. He appears in the Gospels as the supreme Lord of the earth, of demons, and of the supernatural life.

Everything is subject to His sovereign domain.

In this power of the Savior, there is another most secure motive for confidence. Nothing can keep Our Lord from helping and protecting us.

At the very beginning of His apostolic ministry, He assists at the wedding of Cana. During the course of the banquet, the wine runs short. What a humiliation for the people who had invited the Master, His Mother, and His disciples! The Blessed Virgin Mary very quickly perceives the misfortune; she is always the first to perceive our necessities and to relieve them. She turns to her Son with a gaze of supplication; in a low voice she murmurs to Him a brief request. Mary knows His power and His love. And Jesus, who does not know how to refuse her anything, transforms the water into wine! And this is His first miracle.

On another occasion, one evening, in order to avoid the crowds that are assaulting and pressing upon Him, the Master and His disciples take a boat across Lake Genezareth. While they are sailing, the wind becomes a hurricane, a tempest is unleashed, the waves rise, and billows flourish with a frightening roar. The waters inundate the quarterdeck; the boat is going to sink. Fatigued from His harsh toil, the Savior sleeps in the stern, His divine head resting on the cordage. The terrified disciples wake Him, crying out: "Lord, save us, we perish!"[6] Then the Savior arises; He speaks to the wind; He says to the furious sea: Silence, calm yourself!. . . And, immediately, "there came a great calm."

Instantaneously, everything is calm! The witnesses of this scene ask themselves with amazement: "What manner of man is this, for the winds and the sea obey Him?"

Many blind men grope forward to approach Him, crying out their misfortune to Him: "Have mercy on us, O Son of David!"[7]

The Master touches their eyes and, by this divine contact, opens to them the light.

A deaf-mute is brought to Him so that He will lay His hands on him. The Savior heeds this desire. The mouth of the man speaks, and his ears hear.

One day, He meets ten lepers. The leper, an exile in human society, is driven away from the crowds, who avoid his company for fear of contagion; everyone flees with horror from his repulsiveness. The ten lepers do not even dare to approach Our Lord; they stand afar. But gathering together the little strength left to them by their disease, they cry out from the distance: "Jesus, Master, have mercy on us!" Jesus, who on the Cross was to be the great leper, who in the Eucharist was to be the great abandoned one, is moved by that misery and says to them: "Go, show yourselves to the priests."[8]

When those unfortunate ones execute the orders of the Master, they find themselves cured! There were three whom He restored to life. Moreover, after having died amidst all of the disgrace of Golgotha and after having been laid in the Sepulcher, He, by the most marvelous of prodigies, raised Himself on the morning of the third day.

And it is thus that He will raise us at the end of time. He will restore our dear ones, our dead, transformed, yet always similar to what they were. In this way, He will wipe away our tears for all eternity.

Then there will be no more weeping, nor want, nor mourning, for He will have ended the era of our misery.

During the three years of His public life, He sometimes met possessed persons. He spoke to the demons in a tone of sovereign authority; He gave them imperious orders, and they fled at His voice, confessing His divinity!

Jesus Is Lord of the Supernatural Life

He raises up dead souls, restoring to them their lost grace. And to prove that He really had divine power, He cures a paralytic.

To the Scribes that surround Him, He says: "Which is easier, to say to the sick of the palsy: Thy sins are forgiven thee; or to say: Arise, take up thy bed, and walk? But that you may know that the Son of Man hath power on earth to forgive sins, (He saith to the sick of the palsy), I say to thee: Arise, take up thy bed and go into thy house."[9]

It would be good to meditate for a long time on this stupendous power of Our Lord. When it is a question of making this power serve His love for us, the Master never hesitates.

Our Lord's Goodness

The truth is that Our Lord is adorably good. His Heart cannot see anyone suffer without bleeding. This loving kindness makes Him work some of His greatest miracles spontaneously, even before receiving any request.

The multitude follows Him to the desert mountains of Palestine; for three days they forget themselves to hear Him, neglecting the necessities of eating and drinking. But the Master calls the Apostles: "I have compassion on the multitude," He says to them, "for behold they have now been with me three days, and have nothing to eat. And if I shall send them away fasting to their home, they will faint in the way; for some of them came from afar off."[10] And He multiplies the few loaves that the disciples had.

Another time, He is on His way to Naim, escorted by quite a numerous crowd. When He is almost at the gates of the city, He meets a funeral procession.

A young man, the only son of his poor widowed mother, is being carried to his last resting place. Hoping for nothing more from life, she follows in profound grief, lamenting over the body of her son. The sight of this mute pain arouses a strong emotion in the Master; "Being moved with mercy towards her, He said to her: Weep not!"[11] And approaching the bier where the corpse lay, He restores the young man alive to his mother.

You souls wounded by trials, with consciences distressed perhaps by doubt or by remorse, hearts tortured by betrayal or by death: you who suffer, do you perhaps believe that Jesus does not have pity on your suffering? This would be a failure to comprehend His immense love. He knows your miseries; He sees them; His Heart takes pity on them. And it is for you today that He launches His cry of compassion. It is to you, as to the widow of Naim, that He repeats: "Weep not; I am Peace; I am the Resurrection and the Life!"

This confidence, which the Divine Goodness should inspire in us naturally, Our Lord demands explicitly. He makes it the essential condition for His benefits. In the Gospels, we see Him demanding formal acts of this confidence before working certain miracles. Why is it that He, who is always so tender, shows Himself to be apparently so hard with the Canaanite woman who asked Him to cure her daughter? He turns her away several times, but nothing can discourage her. She increases her touching supplications; nothing diminishes her unshakable confidence. This is precisely what Jesus wants: "O woman," He exclaims with joyful admiration, "great is thy faith!" And He adds: "Be it done to thee as thou wilt."[12]

"Be it done to thee as thou wilt." Confidence obtains the realization of our desires. It is Our Lord Himself who affirms it.

O strange aberration of human intelligence! Since we are convinced Catholics, we believe in the miracles of the Gospels; we believe that Christ, in ascending to heaven, lost none of His power; we believe in His goodness, proved by His whole life.

Yet, nevertheless, we do not know how to abandon ourselves to confidence in Him!

How poorly do we know the Heart of Jesus! We stubbornly persist in judging that Divine Heart by our own weak hearts. It appears, in truth, that we wish to reduce Its immensity to our own proportions. We have difficulty in admitting His incredible mercy for sinners because we are vengeful and slow to forgive. We compare His infinite tenderness with our own petty affections.

We can understand nothing of this devouring fire that makes of His Heart an immense furnace of love, of that holy passion for men that dominated Him completely, of that infinite charity that led Him from the humiliations of the crib to the sacrifice of Calvary.

Unfortunately, we cannot say with the Apostle Saint John, in the fullness of our faith: "We have known, and have believed the charity, which God hath to us!"[13]

O Divine Master, we would like to abandon ourselves permanently and entirely to Thy loving direction. We confide to Thee the care of our material future.

We do not know what this future, somber with threats, reserves for us. But we abandon ourselves into the hands of Thy Providence. We confide our concerns to Thy Heart. They are, at times, quite oppressive. But Thou art with us to soften them. We confide our mortal miseries to Thy mercy. Human frailty makes us fear our weakness. But Thou, Lord, shalt support us and preserve us from the great fall.

And, like Thy beloved Apostle who rested his head upon Thy breast, so also shall we rest upon Thy Sacred Heart; and, according to the words of the Psalmist, there shall we sleep in delicious peace, because, O Jesus, we shall be rooted by Thee in unshakable confidence.

CHAPTER SIX
Fruits of Confidence

"Blessed be the man that trusteth in the Lord, and the Lord shall be his confidence. And he shall be as a tree that is planted by the waters. . ."
—Jeremiah 17:7-8

Our Lady of Confidence, Rome, Italy

"Spes Nostra Salve—Our hope, we hail thee!"

FRUITS OF CONFIDENCE

Confidence Glorifies God

The ideal way to eulogize confidence is to show its fruits. This is what we will do in this chapter.

May the following considerations encourage worried souls and make them finally overcome their pusillanimity, teaching them to practice this precious virtue perfectly.

Confidence does not evolve in the more modest spheres of the moral virtues; instead, it lifts itself with one leap to the throne of the Eternal, to the very Heart of the heavenly Father. Excellent indeed is the homage that it renders to His infinite perfections: to His goodness, because it expects from Him alone the necessary help; to His power, because it despises any force that is not His; to His knowledge, because it recognizes the wisdom of His sovereign intervention; to His fidelity, because it counts without hesitation on the divine word.

This virtue, then, participates in praise and adoration simultaneously.

In the various manifestations of religious life, no act is more elevated than these two acts; they are the sublime acts with which the blessed spirits occupy themselves in heaven. The Seraphim veil their faces with their wings in the presence of the Most High, and the angelic choirs, filled with enthusiasm, repeat to Him their threefold acclamation.

In a luminous and most sweet synthesis, confidence sums up the three theological virtues: faith, hope, and charity. For this reason, the Prophet, dazzled by the brilliance of this virtue, is incapable of containing his admiration and exclaims with enthusiasm: "Blessed be the man that trusteth in the Lord."[1]

But the soul without confidence, on the contrary, outrages the Lord. She doubts His providence, His goodness, and His love. She seeks the support of creatures, even to resorting to superstitious practices. The unfortunate soul leans on these fragile supports which will break under her weight and cruelly injure her. And God is angered by such an offense.

The fourth Book of Kings tells us that Ochozias ordered the priests to consult idols during his illness. The Lord became angry; He charged the Prophet Elias to convey terrible threats to the sovereign: "Is it because there was no God in Israel that thou sendest to Beelzebub the god of Accaron? Therefore thou shalt not come down from the bed, on which thou art gone up, but then shalt surely die."[2]

Will not the Christian who doubts the Divine Goodness and restricts his hopes to creatures merit the same censure? Does he not expose himself to a just chastisement? Does Providence perchance not watch over him, so that it becomes necessary for him to direct himself insanely to weak and fragile creatures, incapable of coming to his aid?

Confidence Attracts Exceptional Favors to Souls

"Do not therefore lose your confidence which hath a great reward," says the Apostle Saint Paul.[3] This virtue, indeed, brings such great glory to God that it necessarily attracts exceptional favors to souls.

The Lord declared several times in the Scriptures with what generous magnificence He treats confident souls. "Because he hoped in Me, I will deliver him: I will protect him because he hath known My name. He shall cry to Me, and I will hear him: I am with him in tribulation, I will deliver him, and I will glorify him."[4]

What pacifying promises from the lips of Him who punishes every idle word and condemns the slightest exaggeration! Moreover, and according to the testimony of Truth itself, confidence moves all evil far from us. "Because Thou, O Lord, art my hope: Thou hast made the Most High Thy refuge. There shall no evil come to thee: nor shall the scourge come near Thy dwelling. For He hath given His angels charge over thee: to keep thee in all thy ways. In their hands they shall bear thee up: lest thou dash thy foot against a stone.

"Thou shalt walk upon the asp and the basilisk: and thou shalt trample under foot the lion and the dragon."[5]

Sin is in the front line of the evils from which confidence preserves us. Furthermore, there is nothing more in conformance with the nature of things. The confident soul knows its nothingness, as well as that of all creatures; and it is for this reason that it does not count on itself or on men, and puts all its hope in God. It is suspicious of its own misery; it practices, as a consequence, true humility.

As you know, pride is the beginning of all sin[6] and the beginning of all destruction.[7] The Lord flees from the proud man; He abandons him to his weakness and allows him to fall. The fall of Saint Peter is a terrible example of this.

In the merciful designs of His wisdom, God will perhaps permit trials to assault a confident soul for some time. Nothing, however, will shake her; she will remain as immovable and firm "as Mount Sion."[8] She will preserve joy in the depths of her heart,[9] and, despite the roar of the storm, she will sleep as tranquil as a child in the arms of her Father.[10] She will be allowed to bring her journey to a happy ending, for God saves them who hope in Him.[11] But these are purely negative benefits.

God heaps positive benefits on the man who confides in Him. Hear with what ample poetry the Prophet expounds this truth: "Blessed be the man that trusteth in the Lord, and the Lord shall be his confidence. And he shall be as a tree that is planted by the waters, and that spreadeth out its roots towards moisture: and it shall not fear when the heat cometh. And the leaf thereof shall be green, and in the time of drought it shall not be solicitous, neither shall it cease at any time to bring forth fruit."[12]

In order to emphasize, by an overwhelming contrast, the radiant peace of this picture, we ask you to contemplate the lamentable fate of the one who counts on creatures: "Cursed be the man that trusteth in man, and maketh flesh his arm, and whose heart departeth from the Lord. For he shall be like tamaric in the desert... he shall dwell in dryness in the desert in a salt land, and not inhabited."[13]

The Confident Prayer Obtains Everything

Finally, as one of its major prerogatives, confidence is always heeded. We can never repeat this too often: Confident prayer obtains everything.

The Scriptures recommend to us with very accentuated insistence that we stir up our faith before presenting our supplications to God. "And in all things whatsoever you shall ask in prayer, believing, you shall receive,"[14] declared the Master. The Apostle Saint James uses the same language; he wants us to pray "in faith, nothing wavering. For he that wavereth is like a wave of the sea, which is moved and carried about by the wind. Therefore let not that man think that he shall receive any thing of the Lord."[15]

Now, then, of what faith do the previous passages refer? It is not the habitual faith that baptism infuses into our souls, but a special confidence that makes us hope firmly in the intervention of Providence in given circumstances. And Our

Lord says this explicitly in the Gospel: "Therefore I say unto you, all things, whatsoever you ask when ye pray, believe that you shall receive; and they shall come unto you."[16] The Master could not have described confidence more clearly.

We can have a lively faith, and, nevertheless, doubt that God wishes to favorably accept this or that petition of ours. Are we by any chance certain, for example, that the object of our desire corresponds with the true good of our life? And so we hesitate. This simple hesitation, notes a theologian, diminishes the efficacy of the prayer.[17]

On other occasions, on the contrary, an intimate certainty fortifies us to the point of completely repelling every doubt or hesitation. We are so certain of having been heard that it already appears to us that the grace we are seeking is in our hands. "In view of such great confidence," writes Father Pesch, "God grants us graces that, without this, He would not have given." Indeed, the good that we are asking from Him was not a necessary one; or this good did not fulfill conditions that would oblige God, by virtue of His promise, to give it to us.[18] Most of the time, however, this intimate certainty is the work of grace within us.

"For this reason," concludes the author, "a singular confidence that we will obtain this or that blessing is a kind of special promise that God makes to us that He will grant it to us."[19]

A word of Saint Thomas Aquinas will sum up this brief digression: "Prayer," says the Angelic Doctor, "draws its merits from charity; but its imperative efficacy comes from faith and confidence."[20]

The Example of the Saints

The saints prayed with this confidence, and for this reason God showed Himself to exercise an infinite liberality with them.

The Abbot Sisois, as *The Lives of the Fathers* tells us, prayed one day for one of his disciples whom the violence of temptation had overwhelmed. "Whether thou wishest or not," he said to God, "I shall not leave Thee before Thou hast cured him." And the soul of the poor brother recovered grace and serenity.[21]

Our Lord deigned to reveal to Saint Gertrude that her confidence worked such violence on the Divine Heart that He was forced to favor all her requests. And He added that, in acting thus, He was satisfying the demands of His goodness and His love for her. A friend of the saint had been praying for some time without obtaining any result. The Savior said to her: "I have delayed the concession of that which thou askest of Me, because thou dost not confide in My goodness, as My faithful Gertrude doth. I never refuse her anything that she asketh of Me."[22]

Now finally, behold, according to the testimony of Blessed Raymond of Capua, her confessor, how Saint Catherine of Siena prayed: "Lord," she used to say, "I shall not move away from Thy feet, from Thy presence, as long as Thy goodness hath not conceded to me what I desire, as long as Thou dost not agree to what I ask of Thee." "Lord," she continued, "I want Thee to promise me eternal life for all those whom I love." Then, with an admirable audacity, she extended her hand toward the Tabernacle: "Lord," she added, "put Thy hand in mine! Yes! Give me proof that Thou shalt give me that which I beseech Thee!"

May these examples inspire us to recollect ourselves in the depths of our souls; let us examine our consciences a bit. With a pious author, let us pose the following question to ourselves: "Have we put total confidence in our prayers, a little bit of the absolutism of a child who begs from his mother the object that he desires? The absolutism of the poor beggars who follow us, and who, by the force of importunity, are thus heeded? Above all, the absolutism at the same time so respectful and so confident, of the saints in their supplications?"[23]

The Conclusion of This Work

A conclusion results naturally and imperiously from this short study.

Christian souls, employ all of the means at your disposal to acquire confidence. Meditate much on the infinite power of God, on His immense love, on the inviolable fidelity with which He fulfills His promises, and on the Passion of Our Lord Jesus Christ. However, do not remain waiting indefinitely in expectation. From reflection, pass on to action.

Make acts of confidence frequently. Let every one of your actions serve as an occasion to renew those acts. It is, above all, in the hours of difficulty and trial that you must multiply them.

Repeat frequently the very touching invocation: "Heart of Jesus, I trust in thee!" Our Lord said to a privileged soul: "The little prayer, 'I trust in Thee,' is enough to enchant My Heart, because in it is included confidence, faith, love, and humility."[24]

Do not fear to exaggerate the practice of this virtue.

"One should never fear, in the supposition, of course, of a good life, that the virtue of confidence can be exercised too much. Because just as God, because of His veracity, merits a kind of infinite faith, so also, because of His power, His goodness, and the infallibility of His promises—perfections no less infinite than His veracity—He merits unlimited confidence."[25]

Do not spare your efforts. The fruits of confidence are sufficiently precious to be worth the effort that it takes to collect them.

And if, one day, thou shouldst come to complain of not having obtained the marvelous advantages for which thou hoped, I shall reply to thee with Saint John Chrysostom: "Thou sayest: I hoped and I was not heeded. Strange words! Do not blaspheme the Scriptures! Thou wast not heeded because thou didst not confide as thou should have; because thou didst not wait until the end of the trial; because thou wert pusillanimous. Confidence consists above all in raising up our soul in suffering and in danger and in elevating the heart to God."[26]

"Let nothing disturb you,
Let nothing frighten you,
All things are passing:
God never changes.
Patience obtains all things
Whoever has God lacks nothing;
God alone suffices."
—St. Teresa of Avila

NOTES

Chapter One

1. "Confide, fili, remittuntur tibi peccata tua." Matt. 9:2.
2. "Confide, filia, fides tua te salvam fecit." Matt. 9:22.
3. "Confidite, ego sum, nolite timere." Mark 6:50.
4. "Confidite, ego vici mundum." John 16:33.
5. "Verba quae ego locutus sum vobis, spiritus et vita sunt." John 6:64.
6. "Beati qui audiunt verbum Dei et custodiunt illud." Luke 11:28.
7. "Exi a me, quia homo peccator sum, Domine." Luke 5:8.
8. "Noli timere." Luke 5:10.
9. "Non enim veni vocare justos, sed peccatores." Mark 2:17.
10. "Si potes credere, omnia possibilia sunt credenti." Mark 9:22.
11. "Credo, Domine; adjuva incredulitatem meam." Mark 9:23.
12. "Modicae fidei, quare dubitasti?" Matt. 14:31.
13. "Spes autem non confundit." Rom. 5:5.

Chapter Two

1. "Est enim fiducia spes roborata ex aliqua firma opinione." Saint Thomas Aquinas, *Summa theologica*, IIa IIae., quest. 129, art. 6, ad. 3.
2. "In verba tua supersperavi." Ps. 118:74.
3. Saint-Jure, *De la connaissance et de l'amour de Jésus-Christ*, vol. 3, p. 3.
4. "Dominus illuminatio mea et salus mea; quem timebo? Dominus protector vitae meae; a quo trepidabo?" Ps. 26:1.
5. "Itaque quatenus fides est causa et radix hujus fiduciae, potest accipi fides pro fiducia causaliter, ut quando

S. Jacobus ait: *Postulet in fide nihil haesitans* (I.6). Ibi enim et aliis similibus locis fides aut simpliciter ponitur pro fiducia aut intelligitur quidem fides dogmatica, sed in quantum roborat spem." Pesch, *Praelectiones dogmaticae*, vol. 7, p. 51, note 2.

6. Saint-Jure, op. cit., vol. 3, p. 3.

7. Horace, Ode 3 of Book 3.

8. "Etiam si occiderit me, in ipso sperabo." Job 13:15.

9. Louis of Granada, First Sermon for the Second Sunday after the Epiphany.

10. Ibid.

11. *Petits Bollandistes*, vol. 14, p. 542.

12. Saint-Jure, op. cit., vol. 3, p. 3.

13. "Vanum est vobis ante lucem surgere." Ps. 126:2.

14. "Sine me nihil potestis facere." John 15:5.

15. "Sufficientia nostra ex Deo est." 2 Cor. 3:5.

16. Fr. Xavier de Franciosi, *L'Esprit de Saint Ignace*, p. 5.

17. Saint-Jure, op. cit., vol. 3, p. 4.

18. "Gaudete in Domino semper: iterum dico gaudete... Dominus prope est." Phil. 4:4-5.

19. *Soeur Benigne Consolata Ferrero*, Roudil, Lyons, pp. 95-96. This biography appeared in 1920, with the imprimatur of the archbishop and the declarations prescribed by the decrees of Urban VIII.

Chapter Three

1. "Ideo dico vobis, ne solliciti sitis animae vestrae quid manducetis, neque corpori vestro quid induamini. Nonne anima plus est quam esca, et corpus plus quam vestimentum?

"Respicite volatilia caeli, quoniam non serunt, neque metunt, neque congregant in horrea: et Pater vester caelestis pascit illa. Nonne vos magis pluris estis illis? "Et de vestimento quid solliciti estis? Considerate lilia agri quomodo crescunt: non laborant, neque nent. Dico autem vobis, quoniam nec Salomon in omni gloria sua coopertus est sicut unum ex istis. Si autem foenum agri, quod hodie est, et cras in clibanum mittitur, Deus sic vestit: quanto magis vos modicae fidei?

"Nolite ergo solliciti esse, dicentes: Quid manducabimus, aut quid bibemus, aut quo operiemur? Haec enim omnia gentes inquirunt. Scit enim Pater vester, quia his omnibus indigetis.

"Quaerite ergo primum regnum Dei, et justitiam ejus: et haec omnia adjicientur vobis." Matt. 6:25-26 and 28-33.

2. Prov. 31:10-28.

3. *Les Petits Bollandistes*, vol. 8, July 18.

4. "Numquid poterit Deus parare mensam in deserto?... Numquid et panem poterit dare, aut parare mensam populo suo? . . .Et ignis accensus est in Jacob, et ira ascendit in Israel, quia non crediderunt in Deo, nec speraverunt in salutari ejus." Ps. 77:19-22.

5. Luke 17:21.

6. "Jacta super Dominum curam tuam, et ipse te enutriet." Ps. 54:23.

7. "Dominus regit me, et nihil deerit." Ps. 22:1.

8. "Vanitatem et verba mendacia longe fac a me; mendicitatem et divitias ne dederis mihi: tribue tantum victui meo necessaria; ne forte satiatus illiciar ad negandum, et dicam: Quis est Dominus? aut egestate compulsus furer, et perjurem nomen Dei mei." Prov. 30:8-9.

Chapter Four

1. "Si quis peccaverit, advocatum habemus apud Patrem,

Jesum Christum justum." 1 John 2:1.

2. "Qui sine peccato est vestrum, primus in illam lapidem mittat." John 8:7.

3. "Et remansit solus Jesus, et mulier in medio stans. "Erigens autem se Jesus, dixit ei: Mulier, ubi sunt qui te accusabant? Nemo te condemnavit? Quae dixit: Nemo, Domine. Dixit autem Jesus: Nec ego to condemnabo: vade, et jam amplius noli peccare." John 8:9-11.

4. "Major est iniquitas mea, quam ut veniam merear." Gen. 4:13.

5. "Oblatus est quia ipse voluit." Isa. 53:7.

6. "Amice, ad quid venisti?" Matt. 26:50. "Juda, osculo Filium hominis tradis?" Luke 22:48.

7. "Pater, dimitte illis: non enim sciunt quid faciunt." Luke 23:34.

Chapter Five

1. *Les vrais entretiens spirituels*, ed. d'Annecy, vol. 6, p. 30.

2. Cf. Acts 4:11.

3. "Admirabilis. . . Deus, Fortis. . . Princeps pacis." Isa. 9:6.

4. "Filius datus est nobis." Ibid.

5. "Deus dilexit mundum, ut Filium suum unigenitum daret. Sic enim." John 3:16.

6. "Domine, salva nos, perimus." Matt. 8:25.

7. "Miserere nostri, fili David." Matt. 9:27.

8. Luke 17:14.

9. "Quid est facilius dicere paralytico: Dimittuntur tibi peccata tua: an dicere: Surge, tolle grabatum tuum, et ambula? Ut autem sciatis quia Filius hominis habet potestatem in terra dimittendi peccata (ait paralytico): Tibi dico: Surge, tolle grabatum tuum et vade in domum tuam." Mark 2:9-11.

10. "Misereor super turba: quia ecce jam triduo sustinent me, nec habent quod manducent. Et si dimisero eos jejunos in domum suam, deficient in via: quidam enim ex eis de longe venerunt." Mark 8:2-3.
11. "Noli flere." Luke 7:13.
12. "O mulier, magna est fides tua: Fiat tibi sicut vis." Matt. 15:28.
13. "Et nos cognovimus, et credidimus caritati, quam habet Deus in nobis." 1 John 4:16.

Chapter Six

1. "Benedictus vir qui confidit in Domino." Jer. 17:7.
2. "Numquid, quia non erat Deus in Israel, mittis ut consulatur Beelzebub deus Accaron? Idcirco de lectulo super quem ascendisti, non descendens, sed morte morieris." 4 Kings 1:6.
3. "Nolite itaque amittere confidentiam vestram, quae magnam habet remunerationem." Heb. 10:35.
4. "Quoniam in me speravit, liberabo eum: protegam eum, quoniam cognovit nomen meum. Clamabit ad me, et ego exaudiam eum; cum ipso sum in tribulatione, eripiam eum, et glorificabo eum." Ps. 90:14-15.
5. "Quoniam... Altissimum posuisti refugium tuum, non accedet ad te malum, et flagellum non appropinquabit tabernaculo tuo. Quoniam Angelis suis mandavit de te, ut custodiant te in omnibus viis tuis. In manibus portabunt te, ne forte offendas ad lapidem pedem tuum. Super aspidem et basiliscum ambulabis, et conculcabis leonem et draconem." Ps. 90:9-13.
6. "Initium omnis peccati est superbia." Ecclus. 10:15.
7. "Ante ruinam exaltatur spiritus." Prov. 16:18.
8. "Qui confidunt in Domino, sicut mons Sion." Ps. 124:1.

9. "Dedisti laetitiam in corde meo." Ps. 4:7.

10. "In pace in idipsum dormiam, et requiescam: quoniam tu, Domine, singulariter in spe constituisti me." Ps. 4:9-10.

11. "Salvos facis sperantes in te." Ps. 16:7.

12. "Benedictus vir qui confidit in Domino, et erit Dominus fiducia ejus. Et erit quasi lignum quod transplantatur super aquas, quod ad humorem mittit radices suas, et non timebit cum venerit aestus. Et erit folium ejus viride, et in tempore siccitatis non erit sollicitum, nec aliquando desinet facere fructum." Jer. 17:7-8.

13. "Maledictus homo qui confidit in homine, et ponit carnem brachium suum, et a Domino recedit cor ejus. Erit enim quasi myricae in deserto... habitabit in siccitate in deserto, in terra salsuginis et inhabitabili." Jer. 17:5-6.

14. "Quaecumque petieritis in oratione credentes, accipietis." Matt. 21:22.

15. "Postulet autem in fide nihil haesitans: qui enim haesitat, similis est fluctui maris, qui a vento movetur et circumfertur. Non ergo aestimet homo ille quod accipiat aliquid a Domino." James 1:6-7.

16. "Propterea dico vobis, omnia quaecumque orantes petitis, credite quia accipietis, et evenient vobis." Mark 11:24.

17. "Haec haestatio non quidam tollit, sed minuit efficaciam orationis." Christianus Pesch, *Praelectiones dogmaticae*, vol. 9, p. 166.

18. "Ob hanc perfectionem fiduciae interdum dat Deus bonum, quod alias non daret, quia non erat ita necessarium, vel non habebat alias conditiones, propter quas ex vi solius promissionis illud dare teneretur." Pesch, loc. cit.

19. "Itaque singularis fiducia impertrandi aliquam particularem desideratam est quasi promissio specialis Dei circa hanc rem." Pesch, loc. cit.

20. "Oratio efficaciam merendi habet a charitate, at vero efficaciam impetrandi a fide et fiducia." Saint Thomas Aquinas, *Summa theologica*, II-II, quest. 83, art. 15, ad. 3.

21. *Vita Patrum*, book 6.

22. Saint-Jure, op. cit., vol. 3, p. 27. 23. Sauvé, *Jésus intime*, vol. 2, p. 428.

24. *Soeur Benigne Consolata Ferrero*. Cf. note 19 of Chapter Two.

25. Saint-Jure, op. cit., vol. 3, p. 6.

26. "*Dices*: Ego speravi, et sum pudore affectus. Bona verba, quaeso, a homo! Ne Divinae Scripturae obloquaris. Nam si pudore affectus es, ideo affectus es, quod non, oportuit, speraveris, ex eo quod cesseris, ex eo quod finem non expectaveris, pusillo et angusto animo fueris. Hoc enim vel maxime est sperare, quando in media mala et pericula fueris conjectus, tunc erigi." Saint John Chrysostom, *In Psalm.*, 117.

APPENDIX A

Trusting Through the Dark Night

BY

Plinio Corrêa de Oliveira

Life is a continuous struggle ranging from moments of sadness to times of joy. Indeed Divine Providence gave mankind a sensible sign of this truth in a day's progression from light to darkness, and back to light.

Think of the sunrise. The sun comes up at dawn and increases in splendor throughout the day. If a man did not know better, he could witness this great battle, in which the sun utterly defeats the darkness, and suppose that daytime would last forever. He could even think that the light would never disappear again.

However, shortly after the sun's zenith at noon he would notice that its light is slightly dimmed. Filled with doubt, he might ask: "Can this be? Could a light as bright as the sun really be waning? It must be an illusion, for such a marvelous sun could never set."

In a little while, he perceives that the sun's brightness has further decreased. Nevertheless, he reassures himself: "Well, for such a bright sun, losing a few degrees of brightness is inconsequential."

Later, he again notices the sun's light diminishing. He is optimistic: "It's no big deal that the sun dimmed a bit. I feel tired and perhaps its softening light will help me rest. Surely, this is God's Wisdom. He reduces the sun's brightness to help me sleep.

As night approaches, he takes a walk in the nearby woods and begins to feel nervous. Since, the sun's light penetrates the forest less, night is already moving in.

He looks around and asks himself: "Is this natural? Even though the forest is dark at noontime, I do not think it is normal for the sun to be obscured completely. This cannot be right. I saw the sun in all its glory and beauty and I refuse to believe it is setting." He continues to be optimistic, *Quomodo Obscuratum est Aurum?* (How can the gold be obscured?)

Feeling tired, he sits at the base of a tree and falls asleep. When he wakes, night has set in. The animals that were awake, are now asleep; other animals are now active. They howl and hoot. They fly around in strange ways. Everything seems sinister and he is convinced that the sun has been utterly defeated. He supposes that from now on there will only be darkness.

Back in the field, he peers at the star-studded sky and thinks: "O, no, these are fragments of the sun! Utterly defeated, the sun is now shattered and scattered throughout the firmament. Soon, these points of light too will be extinguished and my situation will be hopeless. I do not know how I will survive in this confused place full of unknown beasts. Even the birds, which delighted me, now fill me with fear."

Then he looks up at an owl and hears: "hoo. . . hooo. . . hooooo!" He thinks: "What is this? What has happened? How did all that splendor disappear? And again, *Quomodo obscuratum est aurum?*' The gold that lit the topmost sky is now obscured and it is night."

The Sun Rises Out of the Darkness

Later he, who formerly misinterpreted the first signs of night, looks at the sky and perceives a faint hint of light. He rubs his eyes and stares again. He thinks: "No, it cannot be. I'm depressed; I've given up. I haven't even the courage to hope. I will drop my head in my hands and cry. I will try to sleep for as long as this darkness lasts. If death comes in this darkness, I will bless death! I will sink into death's embrace and say: 'At least now, I no longer have to look at this darkness that has overtaken everything.'"

He lies down, but cannot sleep. About an hour later, he rises and looks at the sky. Noticing more light, he says: "It's undeniable; I do see some light. . ." Nevertheless, he repeats the false reasoning that he made when the sun was setting: "What can this bit of light do against such lasting darkness? Oh light, you give me false hope. You lie. I refuse to celebrate your appearance, because you are a mere illusion."

Later, as the light continues to increase, he thinks: "Could the light reconquer the darkness once more, just as the darkness conquered the light? Might I see the sun at full zenith once again?" Feeling somewhat depressed over the whole matter, he concludes: "If so, I cannot accept this situation. I cannot bear a life of strife in which the struggle between light and darkness is so intense. Life would be tense, heavy and difficult. I cannot bear it."

He falls asleep again. Soon, amid his dreams, he hears the song of a familiar bird. He opens his eyes and everything is illuminated. He gets up joyfully and thinks: "Now is the sun's revenge. It will not allow itself to be swallowed up ever again. The days of perpetual light have returned."

When night comes around yet again, he says: "This cannot be happening. The night is really in charge here, the day is powerless, night is perpetual. . ."

Such false reasoning would lead such a man to the point of madness.

God Made Night and Day for Man

What is this man's error? First, he does not understand that God's providence rules everything. Even those things that appear absurd and senseless have their place in God's gener-

al plan. For the good of man, God wills light and also darkness, and that light follow darkness.

God made night for man's rest and day for man's joy, an aid
to his work. Night evokes thoughts of death and reminds man
of his own end. Night also symbolizes the instability of days in
the sun and demonstrates that only one thing remains constant, He, Who hovers above day and night, God in His Eternity.

Night and day should teach man that he should put his full
trust only in God, and properly understood, in His Holy
Mother, the Mediatrix of all Graces.

The Need to Fight Gives Life Meaning

The man of our story does not understand that, with day and
night, God created the conditions for man to live on earth. A
world of either perpetual light or darkness would be unlivable,
as would a life of constant joy—sought by so many in our
days—or constant sadness—often preferred to hoping, praying and fighting. Both extremes run contrary to man's nature.

With this rotation of day and night, God demonstrates that everything is fleeting. Since everything can either pass or lead to unexpectedly good results, man must fight.

This fight renders life meaningful. First, man must fight against himself. He must conquer his defects and evil tendencies, which inwardly plot his ruin. He must also fight external enemies. He must also resist the action of the devil and his agents who try to drag man into sin. Man must fight against sickness and poverty. He must fight to provide for his needs. Indeed, man must fight for everything in life.

God Gives the Grace to Conquer

In this life, fighting is the norm without which life becomes unbearable.

God gives us the means to affect these seemingly invariable conditions for our good. He only asks that we agree to fight.

Ultimately, our victory depends upon God's grace, which gives us the agility to identify and crush evil when it first appears in its embryonic form. If we correspond to this grace, we will have brilliant victories and good will reign in us and in society.

**He Who Has Confidence in
Our Lady Will See the Sunrise of Her Victory**

This story should also teach us that when evil appears most powerful and its victory most certain, he who prays to Our Lady with unfailing confidence will witness the sunrise of her victory. ■

About the Author of *Trusting Through the Dark Night:*
Plinio Corrêa de Oliveira

Plinio Corrêa de Oliveira was born in São Paulo, Brazil, in 1908. He obtained a doctorate in Law and was a History Professor at two prestigious universities in São Paulo.

A Catholic man of action, he wrote extensively and had his works published all over the world. He founded the paper *Catolicismo*, and fought the inroads of Communism in Brazil. In 1960 he founded the Brazilian Society for the Defense of Tradition, Family and Property (TFP) of which he was president until his death in 1995.

Inspired by his book *Revolution and Counter-Revolution* and other works, numerous, autonomous TFPs have sprung up around the world.

APPENDIX B

Irresistible Novena to the Sacred Heart of Jesus

O my Jesus who didst say: "Indeed I say to you, ask and it shall be given you; seek and you shall find; knock and it shall be opened to you." Here I am, knocking, seeking, and asking the grace *(mention your request).*

Our Father, Hail Mary, Glory be...
Most Sacred Heart of Jesus, I place all my trust in Thee.

O my Jesus who didst say: "Indeed I say to you, whatever you shall ask the Father in My name, it shall be granted to you." Here I am, asking Thy Father in Thy name for the grace *(mention your request).*

Our Father, Hail Mary, Glory be...
Most Sacred Heart of Jesus, I place all my trust in Thee.

O my Jesus who didst say: "Indeed I say to you, heaven and earth shall pass, but my words shall not pass." Here I am, and supporting myself on the infallibility of Thy words, I ask Thee the grace *(mention your request).*

Our Father, Hail Mary, Glory be...
Most Sacred Heart of Jesus, I place all my trust in Thee.

Prayer:
O Sacred Heart of Jesus, for whom only one thing is impossible and that is not to feel compassion for the wretched, have pity on us, miserable sinners, and grant us the grace which we ask Thee through the Immaculate Heart of She who is Thy tender Mother and also ours.

Recite the Hail, Holy Queen. . .
Saint Joseph, foster father of Jesus, pray for us.